D0478519

Published by Creative Education
P.O. Box 227, Mankato, Minnesota 56002
Creative Education is an imprint of The Creative Company
www.thecreativecompany.us

Design and Production by The Design Lab
Printed in the United States of America

Photographs by Corbis (Andrew Brown/Ecoscene, Gary W. Carter, M. Dillon, David Gallant,
Phillip Gould, Maurice Nimmo/Frank Lane Picture Agency, PBNJ Productions, Carl &
Ann Purcell, Roger Ressmeyer, Stapleton Collection, Roger Wilmshurst/Frank Lane Picture
Agency, Adam Woolfitt), iStockphoto (Duncan Babbage, Timothy Ball, Robyn Koop)

Library of Congress Cataloging-in-Publication Data
Riggs, Kate.
Stonehenge / by Kate Riggs.
p. cm. — (Places of old)
Includes bibliographical references and index.
ISBN 978-1-58341-711-9
1. Stonehenge (England)—Juvenile literature.
2. Wiltshire (England)—Antiquities—Juvenile literature.
3. Megalithic monuments—England—Wiltshire—Juvenile literature. I. Title. II. Series.
DA142.R547 2009   936.2'319—dc22   2007052039

First edition

2 4 6 8 9 7 5 3 1

STONEHENGE

by Kate Riggs

CREATIVE EDUCATION

STONEHENGE is a large circle of stones. It is in the country of England. A ditch called a henge goes around the

stones. The henge was probably six feet (1.8 m) deep at first. But it has filled in with dirt over time.

Stonehenge is one of England's most visited sites

Stonehenge was finished about 3,500 years ago. Scientists think that people called "Beaker Folk" built it. But then the people abandoned it.

Stonehenge is in an area of England called the Salisbury (SOLES-ber-ee) Plain.

The Beaker Folk used metal tools such as these

The Salisbury Plain is a good area for farming

Stones called sarsen and bluestone were used to build Stonehenge. The first circle was made of 80 bluestones. These stones came from mountains in a country called Wales. The bluestones were about 6.5 feet (2 m) tall. Bigger rocks of sarsen were put around the bluestones later. These stones were about 16 feet (5 m) tall!

Bluestone is a hard rock named for its bluish color

It took about 200 years to build the sarsen circle

Some of the upright sarsen stones look like big doorways. Other sarsen stones sit on top of them.

Visitors to Stonehenge are impressed by the big rocks

No one knows why Stonehenge was built. Maybe it was a place where people worshiped their gods. Maybe it was used as a giant calendar. Many people used to think the stones were magical.

Some people call Stonehenge a temple, or worship place

Stonehenge does not look the same today as it did thousands of years ago. Stones have been moved around. Some stones have fallen down. People took some stones when they made buildings nearby.

12

People called Druids sometimes gather at Stonehenge

Visitors are no longer allowed to touch the stones

Some people still believe Stonehenge is a magical place. They gather there at special times.

The Heel Stone is made of a single block of sarsen

Only part of the very first Stonehenge still stands today. But the main entrance to the circle is still easy to see. It faces the direction of the sunrise. Only 25 sarsen stones and 18 bluestones stand upright today.

Stonehenge was built slowly. It took almost 2,000 years until all the stones were in place!

Almost one million visitors come to Stonehenge each year. They walk around the big stones that are still standing. They like to imagine what it was used for thousands of years ago.

Birds like the great bustard and other animals like newts and butterflies live near Stonehenge.

England is home to about 58 kinds of butterflies

Many visitors pose for pictures near Stonehenge

England's wet weather has worn down the stones

People visit Stonehenge at any time of the year. It is damp and cool in England most of the time. People carry umbrellas in case it rains.

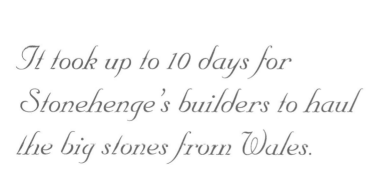

It took up to 10 days for Stonehenge's builders to haul the big stones from Wales.

19

An umbrella is a good item to have in England

Even if it is not warm and sunny, people still enjoy visiting Stonehenge.

A trip to Stonehenge is always an adventure

The strange circle of stones draws people to it. And it always will.

The tall stones stand out against the flat, grassy land

glossary

abandoned
something that has been left behind

bluestone
rocks that were made by volcanoes long ago; they
are blue or gray in color

damp
slightly wet

entrance
opening or beginning place

read more about it

Bernard, Nancy Stone, and Caroline Malone.
Stonehenge. Oxford: Oxford University Press, 2002.

Lace, William W. *Stonehenge.* Farmington Hills,
Mich.: Lucent Books/Thomson Gale, 2003.

index